EVERYONE
LOVES
A
NON~ANXIOUS
PRESENCE

CALM DOWN, GROW UP,
AND LIVE YOUR BEST LIFE

I0617252

EVERYONE LOVES A NON~ANXIOUS PRESENCE

CALM DOWN, GROW UP, AND LIVE YOUR BEST LIFE

BY JACK SHITAMA

CHARIS WORKS

Published by Charis Works, Inc. Earleville, Maryland. Inquiries may be sent to jack@christian-leaders.com.

Edited by Trinity McFadden

Book cover design by Claire Purnell Graphic Design
Interior book design by Claire Purnell Graphic Design

Mandala image: Illustration 23828936 | Symbol © Realillusion | Dreamstime.com

Lavender: 109795408 © Kanlayarawit Boonma | Dreamstime.com

ISBN 979-8-9893554-0-2 (Paperback)
ISBN 979-8-9893554-1-9 (Ebook)

Table of Contents

Introduction

My mother just turned 100. She's an amazing, determined, strong-willed woman. She has supported and encouraged me throughout my life. Even so (or because of this), I had a hard time standing up to her when I was growing up. It wasn't her. It was me. But, as I learned about self-differentiation and began working on myself, I got better at it.

In 2015, our oldest daughter's wedding was held on the Outer Banks of North Carolina. It's a place where our family has vacationed nearly every year since 1990. We rented a big house and made it a week-long celebration.

The wedding itself took place at the end of March. That's an iffy time weather-wise. It can be sunny and warm or windy and cold. On the wedding day, it was not only windy and cold, it was also raining lightly. The ceremony was to take place on a large deck, which faced the ocean.

As the appointed time approached, my mom (who was a spry 91 year-old) kept telling me that we had to move the ceremony inside. I felt pressure to comply. But I also knew about emotional triangles and realized that she was asking me to interfere with my daughter's wishes.

When the moment of truth arrived, I asked my daughter, "What do you want to do?"

Her reply was, "I'm getting married on the deck."

I paused. Then I replied, "Then that's what we'll do." It was settled and everybody went along, even my mom.

I recall this moment because, for me, it was one of those times where remaining a non-anxious presence was not only helpful, it was life-giving. I still have many moments when I don't do as well under pressure, but I believe that understanding the concepts that I share in this book has helped me to do better, especially when it really matters.

I hope they will help you, too. If they do, then you can learn more by listening to my podcast, The Non-Anxious Leader, as well as by going to my website, www.thenonanxiousleader.com.

CHAPTER ONE
The Anxiety Virus

Anxiety is like a virus: It's invisible. It infects you without your consent. Sometimes you know where it came from. Other times you have no idea. It can literally go VIRAL. Anxiety spreads through relationship systems like a silent killer. This sounds scary (but anxiety is scary).

Seth Godin describes non-clinical anxiety as experiencing failure in advance. When you are anxious, you are worrying about a future that has not yet occurred. That's bad enough. Worse yet, anxiety can run amok and make life miserable for you and for those around you. Two things can happen, neither of which is good.

First, anxiety and worry can rattle around in your head, making it hard to function like a normal human being. Not good.

Second, you can be the source of the anxiety virus. You can take it out on other people through anger, blaming, and all-around nasty behavior.

The good news is: you probably won't do this to acquaintances and coworkers (though if you're *really* anxious, you might). It's more likely that you will take it out on those you care about most. This is especially true with family, because that's where you often learned this kind of behavior to begin with.

So, what's the antidote to the anxiety virus? Let's look at that next.

Reflection Questions

- What makes you anxious?
- When and how do you spread it?
- How do you respond when others are anxious, and how do they respond to you when you are anxious?

CHAPTER TWO

Everyone Loves a Non-Anxious Presence

A non-anxious presence is the best defense against anxiety.

A non-anxious presence is someone who connects emotionally with others in a healthy way. They show they care, but not so much that they let their own anxiety get in the way. They may often feel anxious, especially with other people who are anxious, but they are able to regulate their anxiety, so they present themselves as non-anxious. People not only find this calming and helpful (usually), but they also want to be around people like that. Everyone loves a non-anxious presence.

For example, when the mother of the groom is late for the wedding, a non-anxious presence stands close to the father of the bride and keeps him calm. He may be beside himself and want to jump out of his skin, but the non-anxious presence reminds him that there's nothing he can do and that, even if the ceremony starts late, everything will be fine. Everyone else is on edge waiting to see what the father will do. Since he remains calm, so does everyone else.

If you want to be a non-anxious presence, then you need to learn about self-differentiation. This is the ability to be yourself in the midst of surrounding togetherness pressure. What is this? It's the pressure in any relationship system to conform to the norms of that system. Here are some examples:

- Everybody in our family goes to college.

- We don't do family reunions.

- What do you mean you won't be home for the holidays?

Surrounding togetherness pressure makes it hard to self-differentiate, because if you don't want to go along, you end up causing trouble. A non-anxious presence is someone who can do their own thing, even if it doesn't conform, while staying connected in a healthy way to those who are unhappy with their choice(s).

This is not easy stuff, but it's the best way to live. It's good for you, and it's good for those you care about.

It helps to recognize the difference between the emotional process and the content of a situation. That's up next.

Reflection Questions

- Where do you experience surrounding togetherness pressure?

- How do you respond?

- What would it look like to self-differentiate as a non-anxious presence?

CHAPTER THREE
It's Process, Not Content

If you want to be a non-anxious presence, you need to be able to distinguish between the emotional process and the content in any given situation.

Separating emotional process from content is simple, but it's not easy. It's simple, because in any interaction you can ask yourself, "Is something going on in the other person that has little to do with me or the situation at hand?" If so, that's emotional process, or "process" for short.

The content is whatever you're discussing. Let's say two adult siblings are arguing over which presidential candidate is best for the country (this never happens, right?). The content is presidential politics. The emotional process is each sibling's need to be right.

Making the distinction between process and content is not easy because most of us are more likely to speak without thinking. We automatically react to whatever is happening. This is usually reactivity or adaptivity (we'll cover those in chapter 5).

You don't have to understand the emotional process that the other person is experiencing. You just need to recognize that it's happening. Then you'll know you should avoid the content of a situation. The thinking mind is unable to process content while the emotions are in charge. The first clue this is happening is the level of anxiety. If there is a lot of tension and if anxiety is being unleashed, it's possible there is an emotional process issue in play.

Let's say you call your mom to tell her that you've decided to go be with your partner's family for the holidays. Your mom starts crying and tells you that you've never loved her. Her emotionality is a sign that there's something more going on than the content of the situation.

However, this is not always the case. Tension and anxiety can occur even when people are self-differentiating. But tension combined with externalized anxiety is often a sign that the content of the situation should be avoided.

Another clue is whether people are defining themselves or defining others. When they are defining self, especially in a non-anxious way, this is self-differentiation.

Going back to our example, your mom was defining you. She says you never loved her. If she were defining herself, she would say, "I'm disappointed you're not going to be there." She doesn't even have to say it's okay. It can be a situation where there's tension and anxiety, but you're both self-differentiating. You've defined yourself by saying you're going to your partner's family for the holidays. She's defined herself by saying she's disappointed.

It's a tough situation, but you are both self-defining AND staying emotionally connected. It's hard, but this is what grownups do.

Another sign that someone is not defining self is if they are blaming you or telling you what to do. When someone says, "You always...," then it's a good sign they are defining you and not themselves.

The important thing about distinguishing process from content is to realize that emotionality needs emotionality to persist. If you get defensive or argumentative, this will maintain or escalate the level of anxiety and enable it to continue. Likewise, if you adapt and give in without self-differentiating, it will reduce the anxiety in the moment but will also allow the other to avoid taking responsibility, and so the pattern will repeat. In other words, they unload, you give in, and everyone's happy. (Well, you're not.)

Learning to identify emotional process is like learning a new skill. At first things will be hard to identify. But over time you will get better at noticing anxiety, blame, pain displacement, and the lack of taking responsibility for one's own functioning. Engaging with others when they are self-differentiating, even if they don't agree, will encourage healthy conversation and grow your relationship. Avoiding content when people are not differentiating will give them back the responsibility for their own condition.

Either way works and will help you avoid a conflict of wills. Let's look into that next.

Reflection Questions

- How can you tell the difference between people defining self and defining others?

- When does the latter happen in your family of origin, that is, the extended family relationship system in which you were raised?

- What can you do to avoid the content of the situation when the other person is stuck in emotional process?

CHAPTER FOUR

Don't Get Trapped by Your Need to Be Right

Nobody wants to be told what to do.

I'm a good example. When my wife tells me I HAVE to do something, I'm almost certain to NOT want to do it. I know that's immature. I know I am, so what are you?

A self-differentiated person can say what they believe while giving others the freedom to disagree. Instead of telling people what to do, they state their own position without making demands on others. They make statements like:

- I may be wrong, but...

- Here's what I think. You don't have to agree with me.

- This is what I believe. Of course, it's just my opinion...

You can be a non-anxious presence by avoiding a conflict of wills and avoiding the need to be right. When you feel you need to convince the other person that *you're right* and *they're wrong*, you're the one with the problem. A conflict of wills occurs when *both* sides have this problem. This usually results in high anxiety (which is poisonous) and the inability to keep your cool.

You can often avoid this when you say what you believe while giving the other person the freedom to disagree, but not always. Sometimes they have a need to be right. When this is the case, the best thing you can do is not argue, not agree, and stay neutral.

To do this you need to know how to self-regulate. That's the next chapter.

Reflection Questions

- When and where are you most likely to engage in a conflict of wills?

- How easy is it for you to state your own position without making demands on others?

- What would you like to do differently? How would you do this?

CHAPTER FIVE

Your First Instinct Is Usually Wrong

Human beings are wired to act quickly. It helped our ancestors survive the saber-toothed tiger (and each other). Unfortunately, those instincts are not as helpful today as they once were.

When you are faced with a perceived threat, it is usually not life-threatening. It's more often criticism, blame, anger, or defensiveness from another that is *perceived* as a threat. As a result, your mind and body go into fight or flight mode.

The most important thing you can do is learn that your first instinct is usually wrong. Not always, but mostly. When you react without thinking, you are replaying scripts that you learned from your family of origin while growing up.

For example, if your boss talks to you in the same tone that your dominating parent used when you were growing up, you are likely to want to respond automatically in the same way. There are two ways this can happen, neither of which is helpful.

The first is reactivity. This is fight mode. When you are reactive you feel the need to defend yourself or, worse yet, attack the other. Your anxiety becomes a weapon (and it's not pretty). You start arguing with your boss, because that's your automatic response when you hear that tone of voice. That's what you did with your parent, and old habits are hard to break.

The second response is adaptivity. This is flight mode. Instead of fighting, you give in without expressing how you really feel. In this case, you bury your anxiety. The cumulative effect of this is that, occasionally, you can't help but explode to let it all out. This is not good either. In our example, when your boss communicates in that tone of voice, you fold like a cheap lawn chair. You give in, without expressing yourself in a healthy way. It feels bad, but it's your go-to response. Hopefully, you don't blow up at your boss occasionally, or they might not be your boss for very long.

A non-anxious presence is neither reactive nor adaptive. You still feel anxious inside, but you are able to regulate your anxiety. You know your first instinct is usually wrong and have learned how to pause and consider your response. Instead of responding automatically, you are thoughtful and measured. This is self-regulation.

The best thing you can do when facing the anxiety of others (and your own) is to slow things down. Take a deep breath. Close your eyes. Say you need a minute. This will enable you to avoid your automatic response (or at least consider whether it is healthy), then respond in a way that creates healthy emotional space.

Reflection Questions

- How can you distinguish between a perceived threat and an actual threat?

- Is your automatic response more likely to be adaptive or reactive?

- Where and with whom does this happen most frequently?

CHAPTER SIX

Emotional Space Is Like Porcupines Sleeping in Winter

Emotional space is a tricky thing. People need space to be themselves. But without healthy emotional connections, we can't experience life fully. Keeping the balance between enough space and healthy connection is the difference between independence and interdependence.

In his book *Morality*, Jonathan Sacks shares an analogy: emotional space is like porcupines sleeping in winter.

They need each other to keep warm. But if they get too close, they will poke each other with their spines. This hurts. It's not too good for sleeping, either. If they get too far apart, they will freeze.

Emotional space is like this.

You need people: your family, friends, co-workers. But if you get too close, it can hurt. Telling others how they should live their lives or blaming others for your own problems destroys emotional space. This increases anxiety and creates situations where someone is likely to get hurt.

Withdrawing emotionally, disconnecting, creates too much emotional space. We usually do this when we can't handle being connected to others because of the anxiety it creates in us or others. This is not very mature and not very helpful.

Self-differentiation creates healthy emotional space. When you self-differentiate, you take responsibility for yourself and express yourself in healthy ways, without defining or blaming others. People will want to connect because they know you aren't trying to live their lives for them. Everyone loves a non-anxious presence.

The problem is that self-differentiating is hard. Especially because of emotional triangles. We'll cover that next.

Reflection Questions

- Are you more likely to destroy emotional space or to create too much emotional distance?

- What would it look like for you to self-differentiate?

- How can you regulate your automatic reactions?

CHAPTER SEVEN

Triangles Are Fantastic in the Most Awful Way

Self-differentiating is hard because taking responsibility for ourselves and giving other people the same freedom is not natural. Sometimes we want to tell others what to do (and we know how that goes). Other times we don't want to be responsible for ourselves. We want to depend on other people to make decisions or to do things for us. This is not good either (more in the next chapter).

According to Murray Bowen, the founder of family systems theory, the best we can hope for is to self-differentiate 50 percent of the time, and most people do this less than a third of the time. That means that, at best, half of our lives is spent either in other people's business or trying to make our business theirs.

Thus, we have triangles.

A triangle occurs when the anxiety in a relationship between two people makes one or both uncomfortable. Instead of dealing with each other in a healthy way, that is, to express themselves without being adaptive or reactive (see chapter 4), they triangle in a third person or issue.

Remember that boss with the dominating tone of voice? If you give in all the time (adaptivity), you're eventually going to explode. But you want to keep your job, so you're smart enough to regulate that impulse (one for two is better than nothing). When you are mad at your boss and can't express it to them in a healthy way, do you pick a fight with your friend or partner? Or do you complain to a coworker? If so, then you just triangled them. Instead of dealing with your anxiety where it belongs (with your boss), you triangle someone else.

If you don't get along with a coworker and you go to your boss and tell them that they need to fix it, then you just triangled your boss.

If you and your partner are having problems and you start drinking heavily, that forms a triangle, too. The drinking becomes the focus for both of you, which avoids having to deal with your real issues. You focus on drinking to escape. Your partner will likely get anxious and complain about your drinking. Voila! You have a triangle that allows both of you to focus on the drinking, so you don't have to deal with each other (or yourselves).

Bowen called the triangle the most stable form of relationship, because we are unable to take responsibility for ourselves in healthy ways, i.e., to self-differentiate. So, we triangle other people and issues.

Triangles are fantastic in the most awful way.

They are fantastic because they enable us to avoid responsibility for ourselves and our relationships. They are awful because they enable us to avoid responsibility for ourselves and our relationships.

It's important to distinguish between venting and a triangle.

If a friend comes to you and complains about another friend, that's venting. If they ask you to go talk to the other friend and "fix it," then you're being triangled. Don't take the bait. If you get involved in trying to fix the relationship between the other two, you can get stuck for a long time. Plus, you'll be the one who gets stressed out. It's a bad deal.

This leads to another trap you want to avoid.

Reflection Questions

- In what relationships are you most likely to create a triangle to avoid your discomfort?

- What triangles do you recognize in your family of origin?

- Which triangles are only people, and which ones include issues?

CHAPTER EIGHT

Dependent People Suck (the Life Out of You)

A dependent person is someone who doesn't want to take responsibility for themselves. They are unable to define themselves apart from others. They are unable to meet their own emotional needs without the help of another, usually a parent, friend or spouse. Dependent people say things like, "If you don't _____, you don't love me!" Conveniently, they let others take responsibility so they can have someone to blame if things go wrong.

This is the opposite of a self-differentiated person, which is someone who knows who they are, knows their needs, and knows how to meet them. In other words, they take responsibility for self. They are not emotionally dependent nor are they independent. They are interdependent. They can connect with others without demanding that others take care of them. They don't take responsibility for the emotions of others, only their own.

Working toward self-differentiation is hard, but it's worth doing. It doesn't happen right away. It takes time. But it helps to realize that dependent people suck the life out of you. When you recognize the dependency, you can learn how to deal with them in a healthy way.

Reflection Questions

- How often do you act dependently?
- How do you manage the dependent people in your life?
- What might you do differently?

CHAPTER NINE

Your Pain Is Not Other People's Problem (and Vice Versa)

A big mistake we make is to think we can relieve other people of their emotional pain. This does them no favors. In life, pain is an opportunity for growth. The best thing you can do for a friend is stay connected to them and walk alongside them while they deal with their own pain. They will be stronger for it.

No pain, no gain.

Dependent people will want you to take their pain away. They will get mad at you if you don't. You can actually help them by remaining a non-anxious presence. Show you care, but let them deal with their own pain, because you can't do it for them. If you do, they will become weaker. Letting them deal with their own pain is a gift.

The best thing you can do for *yourself* is to understand that when you encounter pain, it is best to lean into it. Embrace it. Think of pain as a friend that will make you stronger. You don't have to go it alone. Connect with others. Let them care for you. But remember that they can't take away your pain for you.

Ironically, the better you get at leaning into your own pain, the more you will be able to allow others to deal with theirs. This will help you to understand that pain and responsibility go hand-in-hand.

Reflection Questions

- How do you deal with pain?
- How well can you tolerate the pain of others?
- What connection do you see between the two?

CHAPTER TEN

You Can't Make Another Person Responsible

Trying to make another person responsible will usually have the opposite effect. This is especially true if you try so hard that you take over for the other. I once heard a mother brag/complain that she was writing her son's papers for him. He was a sophomore in college. This is not the best way to cultivate responsibility.

The best way to "help" another become responsible is to let them experience the consequence of their actions. One time I was grocery shopping and our two-year old son stood up in the seat of the grocery cart. A woman exclaimed, "He's going to fall out and hurt himself!"

I responded, "Only once or twice."

Pain and responsibility are connected.

When we try to take away the pain of another, we make them less capable of growth. When we help people avoid the consequences of their actions, we make them less responsible.

That doesn't mean we don't care about others or even try to protect them. It does mean that we can't do everything for them. The only person you can truly be responsible for is yourself. Encouraging others to do the same, even if it means they experience failure, is a gift.

Taking responsibility for self means owning the consequences for our actions without blaming others. It's going through life without demanding that others fix things for us. It means managing our own anxiety and not putting it on others.

Knowing that change is a part of life will help you do this better.

Reflection Questions

- How often do you try to take responsibility for others?

- What pain are you trying to avoid?

- How might you do things differently?

CHAPTER ELEVEN
All Change Is Loss

Any change in your life is a loss of the old. Bad things like death, job loss, and break-ups create loss. Even positive changes, like a new job, home, or partner is also a loss. The old situation is gone, and you need to adjust to the new one.

With change comes loss, and loss comes with grief. It may not be the kind of debilitating grief that comes from the death of a loved one, but it's still grief.

Knowing this is half the battle. When you understand that any change will create instability in your life and in your family, you have a better chance to remain a non-anxious presence. And everyone loves a non-anxious presence.

This is where it all comes together.

With change comes loss, and that can be painful. Take responsibility for yourself. Own your pain. Work through it. You will be stronger.

Realize that others might be in pain. Stay connected to them emotionally, but let them work through their own pain. Maintain the sweet spot of emotional space.

Understand that with pain may come the tendency to react or adapt to the pain and anxiety of others. Resist that instinct. Regulate your emotions so that you can remain a non-anxious presence.

If you can do these things in the midst of whatever change you are going through, you will grow stronger and healthier. So will the people you care about.

Just understand: it may not be easy.

Reflection Questions

- How do you deal with change and loss?

- How can you use it to grow stronger?

- What can you do to stay connected to others without trying to take away their pain?

CHAPTER TWELVE

Don't Be Surprised If People Are Unhappy with Your New Self

You might think that those closest to you would be happy that you're trying to get better. Whether you're getting less reactive, expressing what you believe in a non-anxious way, or even improving some of your personal habits surrounding eating and exercise, you'd expect your family to cheer you on.

They say they do. But inside something else is going on.

All change is loss.

When you experience personal growth, you are changing. You like the new you. They like the new you (or so they say). But what they (and you) don't realize is that they are more comfortable with the old you.

Because others feel uncomfortable with the new you, they often respond with behaviors that try to throw you off track. Sometimes these are subtle. Other times they're not.

The subtle behaviors tend to occur when you are focused on getting better. Let's say that you've started counting calories and you are doing a great job of eating better and losing weight. Then your father starts complaining to you about your brother and asks you to do something about it (triangle alert!).

This doesn't seem related, but it is. The stress you experience from getting triangled can easily throw you off your new calorie-counting habit. The amazing thing is that your dad doesn't even realize he's doing this. We humans have an amazing ability to mess with others without even knowing it.

These "in your face" behaviors tend to occur when you are focused on self-differentiation. For example, after years of just going along with the family line on gun-control, you decide you can't do it anymore. Before you know it, you're being called a traitor, a loser, and a disgrace to the family (at least you're a triple threat). Instead of defining themselves, they're all about defining you (and how bad you are).

What can you do? Remain a non-anxious presence. Understand that the pushback you are getting is not about you, but is actually about something going on in them.

Remember that there are two components to being a non-anxious presence. The non-anxious part is NOT what you're feeling *inside,* but how you *present* yourself. You will feel anxious. But if you can regulate that anxiety, you have a chance. You don't react defensively or argumentatively, nor do you adapt by giving in to the pressure you're receiving to go back to your old self.

The presence part means you stay emotionally connected. The great temptation when people unwittingly (or purposely) try to throw you off track is to withdraw from them. Why would you want to be around them? But in any relationship system like a family or workgroup, that is the last thing you want to do. Disconnecting from them will only make them more anxious and harder to handle. So instead of moving further away, move closer.

Don't argue. Don't agree. Stay connected. This is simple to understand, but can be hard to do.

Understanding the different kinds of conflicts you may encounter can help.

Reflection Questions

- How do you respond when people try to throw you off track?

- What would help you regulate your anxiety and stay the course?

- What would help you to stay emotionally connected?

CHAPTER THIRTEEN

Not All Conflict Is Equal

There are three different kinds of conflict: Task. Values. Relationship.

Task conflict is when people disagree about how to get something done, who's responsible, or even how to define the goal or task.

Values conflict is a clash of identity or beliefs. Religious and social values fall into this category. When there is a values conflict, progress doesn't occur unless someone changes their mind so that some kind of common ground or compromise can be reached. This is rare. I've learned over the years that people rarely negotiate their closely held values.

Relationship conflict occurs when there is tension or animosity that goes deeper than just disagreements about task or values. In this case, there is a lack of self-differentiation in one or both parties. Relationship conflict is characterized by the lack of taking responsibility for self. This includes blaming the other for one's condition, defensiveness, resentment, and other forms of reactive or adaptive behavior.

When there is no relationship conflict, the other two types of conflict can be handled. In other words, because both parties are self-differentiated, they can say what they believe while giving others the freedom to disagree. Everyone loves a non-anxious presence.

The problem with relationship conflict is that it makes task and values conflict harder to handle. When there is relationship conflict, people confuse the different kinds of conflict. Task and values disagreements are taken personally and can result in deepening conflict and even emotional withdrawal or cutoff. The latter is just as it sounds. The relationship is so damaged that one or both decide they no longer want any emotional connection. They are cut off from one another.

What's important about distinguishing between the different types of conflict is being able to understand how to best manage yourself in the situation.

Ask yourself, "Am I taking responsibility for myself, or am I taking it out on the other person?" If you are taking responsibility for self, then the likelihood is that there is anxiety or pain that the other party is taking out on you. Either way, the key here is to understand the emotional process involved and to avoid getting into a conflict of wills. Don't argue, and don't agree.

The best thing you can do to reduce relationship conflict, as well as task and values conflict, is to maintain an open mind. This is the essence of self-differentiation and being a non-anxious presence.

To learn how to do this, let's put it all together.

Reflection Questions

- Where do you see relationship conflicts in your family of origin or workplace?

- How do you see relationship conflicts confused with task and values conflicts?

- When you're involved, how might you respond differently?

CHAPTER FOURTEEN
We're Talking about Practice

S o how can you put all this family systems stuff together?

Practice.

You **WILL** feel anxious inside. But you can learn to regulate your own anxiety. More importantly, you can use **reflection and preparation** to help you put family systems principles into practice.

Since most of us are only able to self-differentiate a third of the time or less, you're going to mess up more often than you'll get it right. That's where reflection comes in. When those anxious moments occur and you react without thinking, either getting snarky or giving in, it's not the end of things. Take some time after the fact to reflect on the situation. Ask yourself:

- What happened?
- What was the emotional process (not the content) at work?
- How did I respond?
- How would I like to respond in the future?

There is no guarantee that doing this means you'll do better next time, but it will increase the odds greatly. Over time, you will find that you will become more self-aware and intentional in anxious moments.

Preparation involves anticipating anxious situations and preparing yourself to respond as a non-anxious presence. Many (if not most) of these situations occur regularly and can not only be anticipated, but you can also predict how they're going to go.

Other situations involve difficult conversations that you know you need to have. You know what the content of the conversation will be and can likely predict the emotional process at work.

In these cases, ask yourself:

- What is likely to happen?
- How will the other person respond or react?
- What can I do to self-regulate?
- What will be my non-anxious response?

If you can, role-play this interaction with someone who has no stake in the situation. If you can't do that, then rehearse the conversation in your head or even out loud (ignore the stares of those who think you're talking to yourself). Any kind of preparation increases the chances that you can remain a non-anxious presence.

For example, when you know you must tell your family that you won't be home for Christmas, work through what you want to say, such as, "I care about you all, but I've decided that I want to spend Christmas with my partner's family." Then practice saying it slowly and calmly.

You can also think about how you will respond to any pushback you might receive. If you expect you might get statements like, "I thought you cared more about your family," you can prepare yourself to respond with, "Wow! I was afraid I would miss you more than you all would miss me. What a relief." Show you care AND avoid a conflict of wills. Preparation is the key.

As you get better at reflection and preparation, when you encounter anxious situations, you will be better able to:

- Self-regulate to avoid automatic reactive or adaptive responses.

- Avoid a conflict of wills.

- Remain emotionally connected.

- Take responsibility for yourself but not the other.

- Respond as a non-anxious presence in a way that represents who you are and what you believe.

You won't always get it right. But the times you do will move your life in a healthy direction. That will make the practice worth doing.

Reflection Questions

- What anxious situations in your family of origin or workplace are you able to anticipate?

- What would it mean for you to self-differentiate?

- How will you make time to prepare and reflect?

About the Author

Jack Shitama is an ordained United Methodist minister and the Director of the Center for Vital Leadership. He loves to help others become their best through his writing, teaching, speaking and coaching. His podcast, The Non-Anxious Leader Podcast is available on all platforms.

Jack is an avid runner and has completed the Baltimore Marathon three times. He and his wife, Jodi, have four adult children and five grandchildren. They live with no kids and no pets on Maryland's Eastern Shore.

You can subscribe to his weekly newsletter, as well as find more resources, at www.thenonanxiousleader.com.

You can contact him at
jack@christian-leaders.com

Also by Jack Shitama

Anxious Church, Anxious People:
How to Lead Change in an Age of Anxiety

One New Habit, One New Goal:
Change Your Life in 10 Weeks

If You Met My Family, You'd Understand:
A Family Systems Primer

Anxious Church, Anxious People:
How to Lead Change in an
Age of Anxiety Companion Workbook
With Teryl Cartwright

www.ingramcontent.com/pod-product-compliance
Lightning Source LLC
Chambersburg PA
CBHW051647120626
46551CB00015B/2246